The story of a **thrilling escape** from the clutches of the **Sudanese Government's Security Forces**

Dr Daniel A Mamer

ISBN 978-0-6486541-9-3
© Dr Daniel A Mamer, 2019

Published by Africa World Books Pty. Ltd.
(www.africaworldbooks.com)

All rights reserved. No part of this publication may be reproduced, stored in a retrieval system, or transmitted, in any form, or by any means, electronic, mechanical, photocopying, recording or otherwise, without the prior permission of the publishers.

This book is sold subject to the conditions that it shall not, by way of trade or otherwise, be lent, re-sold, hired out or otherwise circulated without the publisher's prior consent in any form of binding or cover other than in which it is published and without a similar condition including the condition being imposed on the subsequent purchaser.

Design and typesetting: Africa World Books

A Note from the Publisher

THE PUBLISHER WISHES TO ACKNOWLEDGE and thank Dr Douglas H. Johnson for his invaluable help and support for Africa World Books and its mission of preserving and promoting African cultural and literary traditions and history. Dr Johnson and fellow historians have been instrumental in ensuring that African people remain connected to their past and their identity. Africa World Books is proud to carry on this mission.

Preface

I FEEL HONOURED to write this preface for the story of a thrilling escape from the clutches of Sudan's government security forces where Mr. Daniel Mamer Ahoc escaped from Wau in 1963 as a young student with nine others on their way to the bush heading towards Congo via The Central African Republic (CAR). Their aim was to become refugees in one of those countries, but the poor young fellow Southern Sudanese were welcomed in the DCR where they found many southern Sudanese refugees in the Refugeecamp. In a state of war, if you decide to fight, you can either kill or be killed, but if you choose to become a refugee you have to sacrifice and face any sort of hardships, so Mr. Mamer with other students took a stern and drastic decision when the country was in a serious political crisis especially, the military dictatorial regime of General Ibrahim Abboud was on the verge to Arabise and Islamise Southerners. This means that they must be made to become Arabs first and foremost and then convert them by means of force to embrace Islam so that, they become Muslims.

For example, Abboud declared Sunday as a working day depriving Christians not to go to church to pray on Sunday and rest as this was the official resting day for them (the Christians). This aggravated the situation indeed and the Christians were left with no option rather to

PREFACE

launch a protest against the military decree. In 1962, Rumbek secondary school students went on strike which became known as "Sunday strike". The students by then acted as the voice of voiceless to air out their grievances against the government of the day.

As a result of the strike, the Rumbek students were rounded up by the government accusing them as instigators and ring-leaders at the same time. Many of them were being tortured badly while in jail and on top of that the school was closed down and many of them were dispatched to their respective homes such as Equatoria, Upper Nile and Bahr-el-Ghazal as these were by then three southern provinces at the time. The closure down of Rumbek secondary school sparked off the crisis as the symptoms of rebellion were emerging to the surface. So the students got this as an opportunity and exploited it as a pretext to find their way of escaping to the bush since they were being targeted by the government of General Ibrahim Abboud. Many of those students who went to the bush were mainly Students from Rumbek secondary and Juba commercial secondary school since they were the only secondary schools existing in southern Sudan at that time. Others were from Intermediate schools and Technical schools as well. It was for the reasons narrated above that made Mr. Mamer Ahoc to leave Rumbek town to Wau lest he may one day be rounded up and arrested by the government

While in Wau, Mr.Mamer was not at ease at all because of fear of unknown. One day Mr.Mamer plus few others just made a decision to desert Wau with his colleagues and went into the thick forest in which they travelled a lot for many days that made them suffered too much from hunger, thirst, disease, bear-footed, nakedness because the few they had worn-out including the little cash they had just finished. It was a very risky journey which was a matter of life and death. They just escaped death very narrowly not only from lack of food and disease

ESCAPE FROM THE SECURITY FORCES OF THE SUDANESE GOVERNMENT

even they had confronted wild animals such as loins, leopards, giraffes, elephants, buffalos, hyenas, and gorillas etc. Also these students met with big snakes of the forest and crocodiles while crossing the rivers full of water to the brim with strong currents caused by heavy rains accompanied by strong storms and so many other hardships in the forests such as hunters whom they fear to suspect them to be government agents sent to capture and hand them over to the government of Sudan. This was the fear they had in their minds.

In fact, everybody in Southern Sudan has a story to tell either collectively or individually not Mr. Mamer alone. From the memorial time to the presence, all Southern Sudanese had suffered a great deal due to continuous instability throughout the ages. To speak the truth, Southern Sudanese had never enjoyed peace for quite a long time since the invasion of Sudan by Mohammed Ali Pasha in 1821 to 1885 the time of Mahdia and the British occupation in 1896 to 1956 when Sudan became independent on 1st January 1956. From Torit mutiny on August, 18, 1955 that culminated to first civil war known as Anya-Nya which lasted for seventeen years. In February 27 to March 3rd 1972 signed Addis Ababa Agreement which granted Southerners local autonomous government by General Jafa'ar Mohammed- el- Numeiri? There was relative peace for eleven years only and again the second civil war broke out in Bor town on May, 16 1983. The reason for this second civil war was because Numeiri had abrogated the Addis Ababa Agreement and re-divided the South in 1982 into three small regions of Bahr-el-Ghazal region, Upper Nile region, and Equatoria region. Secondly, Numeiri promulgated the Islamic Sharia Laws known as September Laws in 1983, four months after the Bor mutiny.

All these points mentioned annoyed Southerners which paved the way for the second civil war that started in 1983 and lasted for

PREFACE

twenty-two years that ended on January, 5th 2005 in Naivasha, Kenya in what is known as Comprehensive Peace Accord (CPA). Therefore, the struggle took Southerners thirty-nine (39 years) in total to liberate themselves from the yoke of Northern Sudanese exploitation, oppression and suppression simultaneously. Lastly, but not the least Southerners attained their independence on July, 9th 2011 after almost four decades of their struggle. So one can just see how the Southern Sudanese have suffered for quite a long time without experiencing peace in their life. Their suffering is not less than the suffering of Jesus Christ, who laid down his life as a ransom for the sake of mankind in order to redeem them from their sins, so I can conclude that Southern Sudanese were born in crises, grew in crises, brought up in crises, became old in crises. Are they going to die in crises? God prohibits.

MAKUR KOT DHUOR
Email : makurkot@yahoo.com.au
August, 6th 2019

Acknowledgements

WHEN I WAS A GRADUATE STUDENT in 1971/72 academic year in Oregon State University pursuing my Master's degree in Agricultural Economics, I had an argument with a Ghanaian Colleague of mine called Seth on trading of raw agricultural products such as coffee beans without any form of processing. Most economically underdeveloped countries or Less Developed Countries (LDCs) sell their agricultural products in this way to the Industrialized countries at a fraction of their value. Once processed, the LDCs buy these processed products at more than three times their raw-state value, thus the LDCs become ripped-off. We call this Economic Colonization or Neo-colonisation. To make us benefit from our products, we have to do some form of processing to add more value to our products. Having explained thus to Seth, he looked at me and said,

"Have you ever thought of writing a book?"

"No," I said.

"Then you'd better because you are so lucid" he said.

My dear wife has also been nagging me ever since I married her on June 31st 1985 that my thoughts are so clear on most issues that it would be a better idea if I begin writing books on some important topics/subjects of concern to society.

I have been reflecting over such comments and the appearance of this book to-day owes much to such extraordinary proddings. So, ever since

ACKNOWLEDGEMENTS

I have been warming up to the idea of writing books. Now I have them lined up. The next two that might come out within the two months or so are: *When you are in Rome, do like the Romans* and *Being a girl in a Dinka Community*. I am also doing a lot of research to write books in my own specialization (Agricultural Economics or Economics of Agriculture, something like applied economics, i.e using economic principles to make efficient trade-offs when dealing with the agricultural problems) and using the Republic of South Sudan as the focus for the analysis, however, these will come much later within the next couple of years.

What prodded me more into writing is the urging done by some of my graduate students some of whom persistently tell me to begin some writing, especially in my specialization so that students can benefit a lot from such an exercise. This has given me more impetus to think much about writing. Because writing is an art that can be learned, I have registered in an institution that teaches writing skills. Those skills plus the desire to write, will suffice to make me effective in being understood by those who will come across my books.

The most spectacular thing that goaded me into writing headlong was to find a publishing company owned by South Sudanese. This company is willing to publish, anything of value that can promote positively one way or another, the people of South Sudan. Most publishing companies can sometimes be discriminative or become exorbitantly expensive. One day when I was near to finishing this book, I began searching for a publisher. I phoned a couple of them which told me that they can publish it, not as a book, but as an article of interest and charging me some sort of a kill-you price. I kept on trying anyway and one day I had a good luck. When I phoned, somebody very friendly picked up the phone. I told him that I had an exciting and thrilling story of escape from the Sudan which I need to be published. He burst into laughter, and I sort of felt that this person must be a South Sudanese. For curiosity's sake I enquired as to who he was, and he said his name was Mr. Peter Lual Reech Deng. I told him who I was, and he said he had heard my name from other people. Instantly, we swished into our local language and had a wonderful conversation after which he told me to send him my manuscript for publication. That made my happiest day for the whole year which I shall always recall. Now I am appealing to all who want to write positively about South Sudan, both South Sudanese or non-South Sudanese to contact Mr Peter Lual Reech Deng through his email and mobile phone which are listed as follows: Email: info@africa-worldbooks.com and the mobile is 0422 611 978. I thank Mr Peter Deng a lot, for being one of the people who thought of establishing a publishing company. MAY THE ALMIGHTY GOD shines upon this company to publish as many books as it can which will make South Sudan be known around the world.

It goes without saying that my daughters, Sarah, Ayola and Alawen kept me happy by providing me with all the necessary and satisfying household services. These services plus the contagious love from their mother, my dear wife, Priscilla Akol, gave me such comfort as to make my work easier and achievable.

Finally all my thanks go to my dear friend Mr Makur Kot Dhuor who has not only agreed to read the manuscript but has also accepted to write a Preface for this wonderful story for our posterity. Mr Makur is the most self-made and self-developed man of any South Sudanese people I have ever came across during the last 50 years.

He comes to this work with a rare knowledge of the human mind and a deep understanding of the book of books, the Bible.

Needless to say, any errors or shortcomings that remain after all the Makur Kot's efforts in reading through the material/manuscript can only be my responsibility.

Introduction

The year was 1963. I had just finished first year in Rumbek Secondary school in early part of December, before Xmas, and was on leave until the end of March 1964. Rumbek Secondary School is found in Rumbek town, the Capital of the then Lakes District of Bhr-el-ghazal Province, one of the then three Southern Provinces of the then Republic of the Sudan. It was the only senior academic secondary school in the whole Southern Sudan at the time. It was opened in 1949, 50 years since the British took over the Sudan as a colonising power. During this period, the Colonial Government had opened hundreds of secondary schools in the North, the region they favoured .The university of Khartoun (UofK) is a multi-campus, co-educational public University located in the City of Khartoum. It is th largest and oldest university in the country. (UofK) was founded as Gordon memorial college in 1902 and established as a full-blown university in 1956 when Sudan got its Independence. Since then the (UofK) has been recognised as a top university and a high-ranking academic institution in the Sudan. Aware that their time for colonisation was almost at an end , they half-heartedly did some small things here and there in Southern Sudan such as taking some Southerners to Police College to become officers, but it was too

ESCAPE FROM THE SECURITY FORCES OF THE SUDANESE GOVERNMENT

little. At this time, that is, in 1963, there was a lot of political turmoil in the country. The Northern-dominated government persecuted Southern Sudanese nationals who were under-represented in all branches of government. The South was being represented by only one minister known as Santino Deng Teng in the cabinet and the Ministry given to us during Ibrahim Abboud regime was that of Animal Resources, as if to say that we were animals. This made many southern Sudanese very angry, especially the educated youth. Some years earlier, one of the administrators- turned politician, called William Deng Nhial escaped and went to Kenya. While there he met some politicians who went before him, especially two of the greatest of our politicians, Mr. Aggrey Jaden and Fr. Saturnino Ohure. The three of them together launched a Political Party called Sudan African Closed Districts National Union (SACDNU) and a military wing called South Sudan Liberation Army (SSLA), nicknamed Anya-Nya or snake poison in Kinshasa. They later moved to Kampala, Uganda, where they changed SACDNU into Sudan African National Union (SANU) in Kampala in 1963. William Deng was also a co-author of a book called "The Problem of Southern Sudan", with Mr. Joseph Odhuo, one of Southern Sudan politicians at the time. The book exposed what was happening in the Sudan. The Government was not very happy about this exposure of the real internal oppressive regime against the people of South Sudan and wanted to kill him, but for that moment he was out their reach. Wild rumours reached Sudan that Deng Nhial got military support from some countries and that he needed young people to start a liberation war. The response was immense, making 1963 the peak year for the exodus. Many young people, the majority of whom were students, went to neighbouring countries of Ethiopia, Kenya, Uganda, and DRC in their thousands, hopefully to get trained as soldiers in order to fight for the session of South Sudan. The rumour was later found to

INTRODUCTION

be untrue, but it did the trick of getting the youth out of the country and to find their way to the bush.

Sometimes William Deng thought of returning to Sudan to popularise the new party and practise politics in the Sudan. He confided this idea to Mr. Aggrey Jaden who flatly refused He told Mr. William Deng that it was not a good idea to go back to Sudan at the time and that he was likely to be killed by the Jalaba (Northern) government. Deng wouldn't listen to his colleague and they departed ways. William Deng eventually returned to the Sudan while Aggrey Jaden remained in exile to continue with the struggle. Eventually Aggrey Jaden was proven right when William Deng was arm-bushed and killed by Sudan Security Forces at Gurman (Abiriu) area, later became known as 'Kubur' William, a distance less than 20 miles between Rumbek town and Cueibet as he was on his way to Tonj. The incident took place on the 9th of May, 1968. William just met his fate while travelling with a good number of politicians that culminated with the end of general election in April that year. Generally, the population was also terrorised by lynching those who are out-spoken or criticised any government policy. The youths are the ones who suffered the most. Not only were they killed inside the country, but they also died while escaping from the country and got lost in the forests as indicated above or died in the battle fields when the real fight for session came.

As for me, as soon as I got my holidays, I went to Wau, the HQs of Bahr-el-ghazal Province which was the venue for most young people in the Province to assemble secretly to plan for their escape to nearby Central African Republic and beyond. Wau is about 138 miles (220.8 km) from Rumbek to the West. So I went to Wau after Xmas. It was very difficult to find accommodation in Wau. But in the end, I found another revolutionary called Thok Ayok, one of my school mates I have known

ESCAPE FROM THE SECURITY FORCES OF THE SUDANESE GOVERNMENT

over the years, who later joined the Movement. He accommodated me secretly. I would spend the whole day out in town and could spend a night in his place and quit very early in the morning each day. This was because if I disappeared suddenly one day without being known where I went, he could be interrogated and might find himself in trouble. The policy of the government at this time was to employ Southern students during the holidays so as not to escape. Experimenting rice growing in Wau area, the Department of Agriculture had a big rice experimental farm in Wau along the river Gadi. I worked there with some students weeding the rice farm near the river while looking for those students who want to escape like me. Each time after work, I would come to town looking for any group of students in restraints, tea-drinking places, where people play card or traditional games where most students go to while away the time and also look for possible candidates who wanted to escape. It was a delicate issue as you have to be careful as to whom you talked to. It took me sometimes to find those who were interested to escape, as we shall explain in the next chapter.

But why were many young people from South Sudan leaving their Country? This is a big question that a non-Sudanese can ask. This was the result of the British Colonial policies they practised when ruling the Anglo-Egyptian Sudan, especially the policy of Closed Districts Ordinance. This Ordinance was the most divisive in the sense that the North and South were treated as separate countries. The movement between the two parts was restricted. If a person from the North wanted to come to the South for any reason, he had to obtain a pass from the authorities stating his name, the reason for going to the South, the time to be spent there inter alia and vice-versa. Then the Imperialists developed the North economically and neglecting the South, creating an undesirable imbalance in education, economic development, inter alia between

INTRODUCTION

the North and South. When the Imperialists left, they simply handed the South in a silver plate to the North and instantly the Southerners realised that there was a 'change of guards' and that they had a new Colonial master who not only began to suppress them, but also denied them any participation in the Government. Undeniably, the Southerners became frustrated and suffered in their own land and naturally they decided to fight and liberate themselves. They started gorilla war after the Torit mutiny in August 1955. The Any-nya rebel forces gradually became more powerful in the bush when the then Emperor of Ethiopia, Haille Sellasie and the World Church Organisation arranged for a peace deal. Signing the Addis-Ababa Agreement on February 27th to March 3rd 1972 by the two parties (the government and the rebels), there was a brief period of relative peace for 11 years. Unfortunately, Jaafar Numieri abrogated the peace agreement, saying that it was not Koran. In May 1983, Southerners went to the bush (in reality a continuation of Anya-Nya re-named Sudan People's liberation Army and Sudan People's Liberation Movement (SPLA/SPLM) and a protracted war of more than two decades ensured. Eventually in 2005, a peace deal was signed that allowed a referendum in the South— that is— southerners were to vote either for separation or unity of the Sudan. The Government of Sudan set very complicated rules for the referendum which if any of them was violated it would result to the cancellation of the referendum. The Government of the Sudan was also to make peace attractive during this interim period 2005— 2010, but according to South Sudanese it didn't do much. Not wanting to give any chance to cancel the referendum, the Southerners followed these rules to the letter and none of them was broken. In 2011, Southerners voted unanimously, more than 98.3% for separation, thus gaining its independence from the North on July, 9th 2011.

CHAPTER ONE

Planning to Escape

It took me some time to find those who were interested in escaping. All this was done in secrecy and with extreme care. The National Security Department in the province was aware that some students were leaving the country to join the Movement. This department employed some young people to pose as those wanting to escape (these young people were moles planted within the youth groups to expose them for arrest at the very time when they were ready to escape). After all your preparations were done and making your last meeting before leaving, the mole would tip off the police and give your venue. Before you could leave you would all be apprehended, including the mole. Within a week you would all be sentenced, but secretly they would remove him as if being taken to another prison and then release him to continue doing the same thing.

Our case was quite different. There was a mole within the Provincial Government who was well known to be a Government loyalist but, very secretly, unknown to the Government, he was actually a rebel. His name was Francis and he had secret agents who identified the real escapees

PLANNING TO ESCAPE

who sincerely wanted to join the liberation struggle. Getting the names of those who are really revolutionaries, the agents would pass the names to this mole in small numbers, e.g. 10-12 people at a time. He would meet with them in a secret place, brief them and send them off to his home village, 100 miles west of Wau on the road to Raga town, close to the border with the Central African Republic (CAR) and 200 miles from Wau, the HQs of the former Bhar-el-ghazal province, one of the three provinces of South Sudan.

In the village he had a younger wife who would receive these guests, give them accommodation for one or two days, then his brother-in-law would take these guests across the border to CAR through the bush to a border town called Obo which was around 150 miles from this South Sudanese village.

Our time came towards the end of June, 1963. We were ten in number as follows:

- Ajal Deng, Primary School graduate and who would have joined Rumbek secondary school.
- Arthur Aquin, Secondary School graduate and admitted to University of Khartoum.
- Daniel Mamer, finished 1st year Rumbek Secondary School and the writer.
- Kawac (?) a trader in Wau.
- Jier (?) a soldier who was on leave from his garrison in the North.
- Matthew Atem Aduol, Secondary School graduate and admitted to the Faculty of Medicine, Khartoum University.
- Mayar Akoon, Law student, Khartoum University.
- Philip Geng, Secondary School graduate.
  I forget the names of the other two guys.

ESCAPE FROM THE SECURITY FORCES OF THE SUDANESE GOVERNMENT

Going on foot and through the forest dictated what we carried. Each of us had two pairs of trousers, two shirts, some underwear, the shoes we were wearing and a blanket or a bedsheet. We gave ourselves two days to wash our clothes and bought a few things like biscuits, soap, some sweets, matches etc.

The day we left, we had decided that we should meet in a particular venue two miles outside the town on the way to Raga at around 7.00pm local time. By 8:30pm we were all there. Luckily we were all Christians so we prayed to God for a safe journey to the unknown world where we did not know what would happen to us. We were to walk all night and just by daybreak we branched to the bush and found a nice, bushy area with a good shade to spend the whole day sleeping.

Of course, we slept by turns, that meant we selected two people to keep watch for two hours, after which another two would take over throughout the day. During the night if we heard any car approaching, we would just disappear into the bush and wait there until it had passed then we rejoined the road and continued with our journey. It took us three days to reach the village where Francis' wife was.

We had planned to stay in the bush all day and then look for our friend's house in the evening but we entered the forest near the village at dawn. A village lady fetching firewood in the bush discovered us and we were scared to death, thinking that she would inform the authorities of our presence. But fortunately, she was the one who later helped us. Explaining who we were, she readily understood and we discovered that she happened to support our cause.

She took the firewood to her house and promised she would come with Francis' wife in the evening to take us to the safe house. Fearing that she might be lying to us and might come with armed Government agents, we relocated some distance from where she found us and left one person as a sentinel hiding on a tree where he could not be seen. If the two ladies came on their own, he would reveal himself to them and we would unite with them and go to the house. But if she came with a male companion, our sentinel would not reveal himself.

Fortunately, she kept her word and she came with the lady to take us to the house. We were given a good safe house to occupy and our presence in the village was kept a secret. In the morning the lady informed us that her brother or Francis' brother-in-law had gone hunting and that he would be back within a week. We waited for a week and during this week each of us contributed a certain amount of money to make peanut and sesame butter to be put in some empty milk cans. The women made a fine job and each of us got a can full of either a peanut butter or a sesame paste/butter. This became very useful for us in the bush. We waited for one week. When the man didn't turn up, we decided to risk going through the bush on our own.

CHAPTER TWO

A risky journey through the forest to the Central African Republic

ONE WEEK HAD PASSED and there was no sign of Francis's brother-in-law, making us to be worried. Every day, some government agents would pass through the village from Raga to Wau and vice-versa and we would be scared that one villager might inform them of our presence, but fortunately, nothing of the sort happened. This meant that most of these villagers were supporters of the Movement. Around July, 10th 1963, we made a meeting in our tukul/hut and we decided to continue with our journey to CAR and beyond. There was a little problem though; Ajal Deng and myself were the youngest, we were below 20 years old (teenagers) each while the rest were either in their late twentieth or early thirtieth. They were worried that if things became tough in the bush; we might not have the necessary stamina to continue and might be the earliest victims. Their advice to us was that

A RISKY JOURNEY THROUGH THE FOREST TO CAR

they would contribute the remaining Sudanese pounds they had (because this money would be useless in the bush), we would buy some chickens, as businessmen, return to Wau and sell them, and then waited when the schools re-opened, we would normally continue with our education. We vehemently refused this alternative, saying that in any revolution, there are casualties, and if we collapsed due to hunger or any other unforeseen difficulties in the bush, then let it be. We were very determined and so they let us continue with them.

That afternoon we informed the lady responsible for us that we would be leaving at around 9:00pm that night. She was very worried and blamed her brother for having delayed to come home from his hunting. Reports had it that some two months earlier about 20 south Sudanese who had wanted to join the Movement got lost in this forest trying to reach CAR and were found dead. In another development, there are many rivers in this forest that are full to the brim due to heavy rains that occur in the months of June to September. These rivers were teaming with snakes and crocodiles and while looking calm and placid on the surface, they had very strong currents beneath the water and if one is not a good swimmer, one run the risk of drowning. In fact, during the last dry season, some hunters found some human bones in the dry beds of these rivers. Briefing us with these tragic events in the forest, she told us that we should surrender ourselves to Lord Jesus Christ to take care of this dangerous journey. She asked her women friends to help her prepare dinner for us.

Finishing dining at 8:30pm., she told us to make a queue in front of her, standing with her legs astride. This is a typical African tradition of wishing somebody good luck when they take certain risks. Telling each of us to crawl between her legs, get up at her back and never look back as you begin to leave her. Each of us did this, after which she

ESCAPE FROM THE SECURITY FORCES OF THE SUDANESE GOVERNMENT

said loud without looking at us "Lord Jesus and my motherhood will keep you safe in the bush until you reach your destination without any harm". Heading towards Raga, a hundred miles away from this village, we travelled all night following the highway and when it dawned we branched to the bush as usual to spend our day sleeping. Our plan was to get as close as possible to Raga town, so that we could follow the road joining Raga to the border town of Obo in CAR. This was not to be, because at the second night of our journey, there was a heavy rainfall, forcing us to take shelter in the first house we found by the road side. Welcoming us at his house, the owner was surprised to have 10 young people drenched through by the rain travelling on foot throughout the night. The first thing he did was to build a huge fire in one of his tukuls/huts. We took off our clothes, remaining only with our under wears. We rinsed our clothes and we spread them to dry by the heat of the fire in the room. The second thing he did was to ask his wife if there was enough food for ten people. It was too late to cook anything, so she roasted for us some fresh peanuts (ground nuts or g/nuts). Our host was suspicious as to why we travelled on foot. We told him that our car broke down and because of the rain we had to find a place to shelter from the rain, leaving the driver and his assistant to fix the car after which they would pick us up on the way.

Very early the following morning, our host was not there when we awoke at 7:00am. And the rain was drizzling. His wife, we were told by the neighbour, had gone to the farm to harvest peanut, before she comes back to prepare some breakfast or us. A Good Samaritan from the village, who was a supporter of the Movement tipped us off that our host was a government informer and that he could have gone to Raga town to inform authorities of our presence and advised us to leave as soon as possible. Dressing our half-wet clothes quickly, we said good bye to our informer and vanished into the bush towards CAR. Those villagers who saw us were shocked and realised that we were rebels. We knew that none will follow us as they thought that we might be armed. Travelling the whole day through the forest, we reached as far as we could from the village. At around 6:00pm., we found a nice low hill on which we camped. Building a huge fire in the middle around which we slept, we built smaller ones some distance from us in a circle so as to act as a deterrent from any attacks by wild animals. Fires scar away wild animals at night, as attested by Africans throughout the ages. Before going to sleep we would have a lot of conversation on all types of topics such as politics, our families, what will eventually happen to us etc.

This was our first night in the bush, and after we settled around the fire, we deliberated on a number of things. Our first concern was to have our small government, so we chose our President and his assistant or deputy. The idea was that if we were to meet any authorities, the president would be our spokesman assisted by his deputy. The second thing was that we had to identify certain wild fruits and wild mushrooms which can assist us to survive in the bush. Our big brothers knew the poisonous wild fruits and wild mushrooms, so we were safe. Moving through the forest all day, we were able to collect these wild fruits and mushrooms. In the evenings, when we had built our fires and sat around them, we roasted our mushrooms which became like meat, a very nutritious food indeed. The President divided the mushrooms and the wild fruits between us, making sure that the youngest members of the group, Ajal Deng and myself, got the biggest share. South Sudanese people are very protective and take good care of their young ones, especially during hard times. Not knowing how long we would remain in the forest, we decided that we consumed one container of our g/nuts and sesame butter at a time. Mr. Jier, the soldier, had a medium-sized spoon, the only spoon the whole group had. The President would scoop a spoonful of this paste for each person, the two young ones (that is myself and Ajal Deng) had a spoon and a half each, —i.e.— eleven (11 spoons) a day of the peanut butter or sesame/butter. After eating the wild fruits and mushrooms, the butter was our last ditch, something like a dessert, before we retired to our floor-beds. It was real good.

What we did not know was that this forest was teaming with wild animals. It was like a very huge national park. There were lions, buffaloes, giraffes, all types of antelopes, elephants, leopards, all types of monkeys, and very huge gorillas, and that was the first time for me to see a gorilla. It was surprising that none of these animals was aggressive. They would not attack unless they were bothered. The monkeys, the closest to humans, would look at us curiously for a long time as if they wanted to identify us and making weird noises. We thought this was because we looked weak due to hunger, fatigued with hollow cheeks as we were very thin. To our great surprise, they really had compassion for us. It was also for me to know for the first time that animals, like us humans, have feelings. Sometimes, after we had built our fires just before dusk, different types of animals would pass in a long line some distance from us, stopped for a while and gazed at us seated around our big fire, the short ones would stand on their hind legs to have a better view of us, after which they would shake their heads and continued on their way to their normal place of sleep. Having rains at night is a regular feature of tropical lands. These were terrible days for us. Our big brothers would be standing around the fire with our blankets spread over their heads to prevent the rain from extinguishing our fire while we the young ones would be putting more dry wood to make the fire bigger. At the end of each rain at night, we would be left wet, but the fire would make us warm and dry in a short time before starting our journey each following morning.

A RISKY JOURNEY THROUGH THE FOREST TO CAR

Our fifth day in the bush was very interesting and dramatic. Lying in the afternoon shade of a very big mahogany tree that could have been more than 500 years old, we felt really comfortable to rest in this nice cool shade. The trunk was so big that it made us interested to measure its girth. It took six(6) of our big guys standing in a circle around the trunk with their chests pressed against the trunk and their arms outstretched to touch each other's finger tips to measure its girth. For us that was the biggest mahogany trunk we had never seen anywhere in South Sudan. Of course, this is undisturbed area, as there is very little human activity here except hunters who are only looking for wild meat and honey. Lying on the soft grass in a circle in this shade, exhausted and hungry, we were shaken by a loud noise of something falling from the sky in our midst. Within seconds, we had run away from where we were lying to different directions, each of us thinking that the government agents have been following us and had now shot at us with a big gun. Luckily, we had a soldier with us, Mr. Jier. He ran quickly and hid himself behind a big tree in the bush, not far from where we laid, hoping to see some soldiers advancing. He didn't see anybody advancing, but instead, he saw a very big fish still alive zigzagging on the ground where it fell and at the same time saw a big eagle flying in and trying to retrieve it. He rushed to where the fish was and forced the eagle to turn away and secured the fish. Blowing the whistle, he got our attention and we returned to our previous place. We found Mr. Jier smiling and said that God had provided us this big fish for a number of meals.

Let's rehearse what could have happened: The eagle could have got this big fish from one of the numerous rivers in the area teaming with fish, and was now heading to its base to enjoy the fish with its family, its eaglets and husband (the eagle could also have been a male, we didn't know, but in most cases the females are the best hunters). Maybe the skin of the fish was not properly hooked to its big claws, and by the time the eagle was just flying over us, the skin of the fish might have snapped under its weight and the fish fell to our delight. Our matches were spoiled by the rain and we had to find a way of making fire. In Africa generally, we have a tree from which fire could be made (I don't know the name of this tree in English language) which we found quickly as there was a lot of it here in this forest. We got a dry small branch of this tree the size of a big toe, about 8"(inches) long, make a small groove on this one in the middle and find another small branch the size of the last finger, about half a ruler in length, clean all of its length properly with one end of it very smooth. You get a dry grass, crash it to be very soft like paper, place the big dry branch on the dry grass with its grooved part up, place the smoothed end of the small branch in the groove in a perpendicular way, press it down hard and begin to rub hard with your two palms. If you rub it hard for less than two or three minutes, there will be a powdery substance very fine indeed that will ooze out of it and fall on the soft grass very hot. When this substance comes into contact with the air it will become fire and on touching the dry grass it turns into flame. Adding more dry grass and dry twigs, you would have made the fire in the bush.

We did our fire as described above, and with our small knives and a small spear our soldier Mr. Jier had, we cut off the head, adding some few centimetres of flesh behind the head. While we were roasting the head, we cut the rest of the fish into long thin pieces of flesh separating it from the middle bone and leaving it uncut at the tail. On each side of the big middle bone we had eight (8) long pieces hanging from the tail, a total of sixteen (16 pieces). We used some fresh branches of trees to make a rack over the fire on which we put our fish to get some heat over night. Cutting some fresh grass and spreading it on the ground to act as a big plat, we placed on it our roasted head. We sat around it and we gleefully

A RISKY JOURNEY THROUGH THE FOREST TO CAR

consumed it and by the time we were all full, there was a balance of it left over. We retired to our floor-beds and slept soundly. Eating the balance of our roasted head the following morning, we continued with our journey well-pleased with ourselves.

Our next episode was the most dangerous and dramatic one. We had four uneventful days where nothing happened, moving and sleeping routinely and monotonously through the forest until we came upon a small river one morning. That was the 10th day since we began our forest journey. We prepared ourselves to cross the river walking in a straight line. On the other bank of the river, there was a small low hill ahead of us. The river was shallow, but literally full of fish as we stepped on them while others were knocking themselves against our legs and thighs to our delight. We were talking wildly on how we would scoop out of the water a lot of fish on to the bank with our bed sheets and blankets. We would have spent some days and ate a lot of fish which could have restored our health, weight inter alia. At this time our sesame and peanut pastes had finished and we were just feeding on wild fruits and our big dried fish which was almost finishing. Reaching the other bank, Mr. Philip Geng, the man in front of us was just about to come out of water, suddenly we heard the hoofs of an animal speeding towards our direction from behind the hill. Just in seconds before we could figure out what it was, there was a huge fat male buffalo standing in front of Philip who was just about to come out of the river. It caught a break in front of him standing on its legs spread out with its head down, and making weird frightening noises coming out of its big belly while its tail was standing erect in a perpendicular way with small movements at the tip of the tail. In a period of about two to three minutes, the world was holding its breath. We felt as if there was no air and we likened ourselves to motionless rats shivering violently with bulging eyes in front of a big cat.

licking its mouth, hoping to be jumped upon by the cat. Traditionally, we know that if the buffalo is in that state it is extremely angry and any slight show of fear will make it jump on you. So Mr. Philip just did that. He knelt down in shallow water and holding his left hand up as a shield, he held a knife in his right hand and looked squarely into the eyes of the wild buffalo, that is, they were face to face with each other. He told us later that the buffalo was looking into his eyes and then winked at the blade of a small knife. The animal must have calculated that this must be a secret weapon more powerful than it looked, and so kept its cool.

Taking good care of the young as our tradition demands in times of danger, our president, Mr. Mayar Akoon, after around three minutes, motioned at us to get away from the line and wade back slowly from where we had come and whispered to us to climb the big tree that was there. (myself and Ajal Deng, were the youngest as stated above). It took us barely two minutes and we were up on the tree. Then Mr. Philip slowly stood up with his eyes fixed hard on the eyes of the buffalo, and the whole group began wading back slowly towards where we had come. They also climbed the big tree. Surprisingly, the animal stood where it was. Our soldier, Mr. Jier had a small whistle. When he blew it, it made the animal so wild, and to our surprise, it rushed to the tree on to which we had climbed and within seconds, it was dancing underneath the tree. Getting tired of dancing, it looked at us, showing its big gum. It went slowly to drink the water nearby in the river, came back and lied down under the tree and began chewing the cuts. Staying there for about one hour, it got up and seemingly moved away slowly. While doing so, it kept turning and looked at us on the tree. It went as far as about a kilometre from us, as we watched it from our vantage point on the tree. Mr. Jier, our soldier, just got down to urinate, while we up there, were watching the animal. All of a sudden, the buffalo made an about-turn and began galloping like a horse towards our tree, reaching it in seconds just after Mr. Jier had climbed the tree. It began dancing like before, after which it lied down to chew the cuts. Repeatedly, it continued this scenario up to 4:00pm when it finally left us alone. We climbed the tree at around 10:00 am; we spent a total of 6 hours on the tree. To be on the safe side, we spent another half-hour on the tree, scanning the whole area properly. Forgetting our previous plan for fishing, we climbed down as fast as we could, crossed the river, and hurried away as fast as our wobbling legs could carry us. Reaching six kilometres away from the river, we camped for the night.

The following day we proceeded as usual on our movement through the forest westwards. Our fish, sesame & peanut butter had all finished. We were just feeding on mushrooms and wild fruits. Three days went and nothing eventful happened. We just pushed on and on, getting really weaker by the day, but we persevered. On the 13th day of our journey in the forest, we came upon a delivering female buffalo by noon time. It was standing while the baby was hanging from its ass, forcing it hard to let it drop down. We had to hurry away quickly from it because if the baby had dropped down while we were nearby, it would consider us a danger to its newly-born baby and therefore could have attacked us. We went our way and left it alone to continue with delivering its baby.

Our most excited day was the 27th.July 1963, exactly the 18th. day of our journey, in the forest. In the afternoon of this day, we came upon a clearing where maize and beans were freshly grown and there was a lone hut with some clothes that are hung out on a string to dry. There was no soul to be seen in the vicinity of the hut whose door was open. We quickly decided that the rest of us would hide in the bush nearby while our soldier, Mr. Jier would, go and check. He went and checked everything: there was a big bed, a big sponge mattress, a mosquito net, some cooking utensils such as plats, cooking pots, spoons, forks, some fruits on the table etc. He had cooked a very big Acida and some soup made of wild meat cooked with some vegetables, neatly covered. Our soldier just looked at these, but never touched them. He came back to report to us. We immediately and rightly assumed that the man was a hunter and that he would be back soon from his hunting. So we just sat hiding in the bush and waited for him. He had found our tracks in the forest and was wondering what so many people were looking for in the forest. He followed our tracks leading to his place. In About 45 minutes later, he appeared on the clearing and he stood in the clearing looking around carefully in the hope that he might spot us, but without avail. He continued to his hut, entered it, checked everything and found everything was o.k as he left it. While the hunter was looking around standing in front of his hut, Mr. Jier, our soldier, who was hiding in a separate bush appeared and walked towards the hut. He spotted him immediately and waited for him. Meeting him in his compound, the hunter was so shocked to meet a man so thin with hollow cheeks. There was a communication problem since we were now in CAR, a French-speaking country. The hunter was a little literate, mentioning a few French words, but mostly speaking his dialect, while Mr. Jier spoke Dinka mainly, some Arabic and English words and since that didn't work, they resorted to sign language using the hands. The hunter was wondering why he was alone and when our soldier realised that the hunter was harmless, he blew the whistle and we all came out and marched to where they were standing in the compound. Seeing how ragged and skinny we were, the hunter broke down and wept terribly, as he must have seen us as walking bones. We were very surprised to have met such a compassionate man. Realising that we could not eat solid food because our stomachs have shrunk, he just boiled a lot of meat so that we only drank hot soup.

A RISKY JOURNEY THROUGH THE FOREST TO CAR

Drinking this hot soup left us sweating like a wet poodle. It was really exhilarating. We had a sound sleep in his compound around a big fire.

The following morning, he accompanied us to the main road linking Raga town, in South Sudan and Obo town in CAR. If there was no security risk, we would have come to Raga town first, and then followed this road to Obo, but because of the insecurity we had to use the longest route through the forest to Obo. On reaching the road, the hunter told us to follow the road to the town which was just around 10 kilometres away according to him. Saying good-bye to each other, the hunter returned to his hunting place and we proceeded to town. Each time we found a village along the way to town, there would be a lot of commotion. Looking at us as walking bones and filled with compassion, villagers rushed to us with lots of food items such as bananas, peanuts, cooked food etc and asked us to eat. The women were particularly touched as some of them were wailing, some crying, while some were trying to put some food in our mouths to eat, and yet some just stood there with tears running down their cheeks. We could only take liquid food from them. It was quite an experience that amazed us as to how human kindness, sympathy and compassion can easily flow forth. We passed three villages and the same scenario took place and at last we reached the town. Before the town, there was a river without a bridge. On the bank of the river was the Home of a big local chief, who was also a member of National Parliament (Assembly). Seeing us in such a ragged state as he was seated on a big chair under the shade of a group of mango trees in his compound, he sent his bazingiir (security guards) to call us and join him. When we arrived, he ordered that 10 chairs be made available. Ensuring that we have been seated properly, he ordered that tea/coffee and water be brought to us. After finishing the refreshments, he began interrogating us. He spoke a little bit of English which was good since none of us spoke French.

ESCAPE FROM THE SECURITY FORCES OF THE SUDANESE GOVERNMENT

We told him everything that we were refugees and running away from persecution emitted to us by an Arab-dominated government in the Sudan. That made him really mad and he told us that he was aware of such mistreatment of the African people by the so-called Arabs in the Sudan. He really sympathised with us. Realising that we were so weak due to near starvation in the forest, he advised that we should spend the night in his house and that he would take us in the morning in his own care to the police station in town. Agreeing to that wonderful suggestion, he ordered his people to prepare 10 huts as there were so many huts surrounding his big mansion, each furnished with well-prepared beds with sponge mattresses, clean bed sheets, pillows, towels etc. Receiving word that all was ready, he told "us to go to our huts, change clothes, give dirty clothes for washing, go to the bathrooms , have a good bath and go back to the rooms and have a good rest". We were amazed at his hospitality. When we had retired to our huts, he ordered his wives to cook a lot of food for us. After three hours of resting, we were invited into a large family dining room. Never had we seen such abundance of cooked food laid on the table on entering the room since we left Sudan. After seating ourselves around the table, Honourable Francisco (the name of our host) blessed the food. He advised that since our stomachs had shrunken in the bush, we should take a lot of soft/fluid food and less solid food for the moment. So, we drank a lot of vegetable soup, fish soup, meat and chicken soup with a little bit of meat and Acida. We were really full of food when we slowly moved to our huts.

After breakfast the following morning, he took us in his big car to town. We crossed the river with a faluga (a big boat that can take some cars and a good number of passengers and ferry them across the river). On arriving to the Police station, the officers were amazed with this surprised visit of his Honourable with a load of seemingly-starved

A RISKY JOURNEY THROUGH THE FOREST TO CAR

and ragged-looking people. He took a salute from them and told them that the government should take care of us and treat us as refugees with all the normal services given to refugees. Having said that to the local authorities, he bade us farewell. While the Police was interviewing us, asking our names inter alia, I just collapsed. I couldn't remember what exactly happened, but I recalled that I couldn't see anything except what seemed to be like a big white sheet of cloth that surrounded me up to the sky blocking my view of anything else, and I found myself on the ground. My colleagues and some policemen acted very quickly. I was taken immediately to the nearby hospital where I was found to be lacking a lot of essential nutrients according to the French doctor on duty. I was immediately put on a drift and my meal for the following two days was sardines full of fish protein. Opening my eyes three hours later, I was surprised to find myself in the hospital. Seeing myself with my friends around me with worried faces, I enquired what happened and they told me what took place. Realising that I had eventually recovered, they were really relieved and were all smiling, including me, knowing that the danger had passed. One of my compatriots was left with me in the hospital while the rest went back to the Police station to finish the arrangement for our accommodation. They went to the market with some local officials to buy some cooking utensils, some food to cook for the night and were then taken to our rented place. After they had eaten their evening meal, they came to see us in the hospital in the evening. At the end of seven days, I was released from the hospital in a good condition.

We spent the whole of August 1963 in Obo town to have a complete recovery and thinking of what to do. There were not that many South Sudanese in CAR, Zaire or the current DRC was the centre of our activities, and so we decided to go to DRC. We left for DRC in the first week

ESCAPE FROM THE SECURITY FORCES OF THE SUDANESE GOVERNMENT

of September, 1963. By the third week of September, we found ourselves in Uele province, North-eastern part of DRC bordering the Sudan. We had to go to Isiro city, the capital of the province situated on the banks of Uele river, to receive some assistance from UNHCR.

While we were there a very strange event took place. One evening, we had a strange visitor who was a South Sudanese. He struck a strange conversation with us, saying that he had just flown in from Khartoum and that he was a Sudanese government employee, telling us lies to feel big and important. The poor guy was not aware of the state of mind of people who had just run away from persecution. We had a lot of paranoia. We just suspected him of having been sent by the Khartoum government to find our whereabouts, so that they could do us some harm. The deal was sealed. We just decided to do some harm to him. We cajoled him into our large single room, tied him up and started beating him. We had a divided opinion: some of us wanted his throat slit with a knife until he died and just dropped his body into the Uele River just some metres from our lodging place. Not sure of his being a government agent, some of us advised caution, saying that it would be wrong to take a human life when we had no proof that he was actually a government agent. The opinion of this group carried the day and so we decided to torture him and let him go. Landing on the man with lot of anger, we really tortured him. Those of us who were smokers put cigarette buds on his hears, face, chest, legs and thighs while others were giving him terrible blows on his head, cheeks and trunk and still others were beating his buttocks and legs with their belts and sticks. At day break, they put him outside our house and let him find his own way. The poor guy could hardly walk.

What we didn't know was that this guy's sister was married to a Congolese lawyer who was a government judge in Isiro city. Arriving to his sister's house, the sister just couldn't understand what happened to her brother. His face and head were terribly swollen, his body full of scars and burns made by cigarette buds. It was a horrible sight for the sister who gave a big loud cry and dropped herself to the floor. The husband rushed to where she was and saw his brother-in-law in such an awful and dreadful condition/state. He enquired what happened and who did this, and he was told that the Sudanese refugees were responsible for this action. He took his brother-in-law to the hospital where he was admitted for the treatment of his wounds. While he was in his office that day, he issued a warrant of arrest for us. While we were enjoying our lunch in our compound, we noticed that our house was being surrounded by armed police personnel. All the 10 of us were rounded up, roughly handled, beaten, hauled into police van and driven to police station for interrogation. Our Congolese neighbours were shocked and wondered why the police were treating us so brutally. Being completely in the limbo, we could not connect what happened the night before and our arrest. What seemed obvious to us was that the Khartoum government must have made a deal with the Congolese government to round up south Sudanese refugees and return them to Sudan. After the interrogation in the police station, we were locked up in prison for the night.

The following day, we were arraigned in court for attacking an innocent man. The man was brought and identified us as his attackers. We were found quilty and sentenced to 3 (three) months' imprisonment for this misdemeanour. This was the first time I ever saw what is called prison. Every morning we would be taken out to cut grass or sweep some parts of the town such as the market place inter alia. Our health deteriorated within a few weeks because we had frugal meals, fatigued due to lack of sleep because the prison rooms were very dirty, full of bugs, annoying insects and very smelly because prisoners urinated in the rooms.

ESCAPE FROM THE SECURITY FORCES OF THE SUDANESE GOVERNMENT

Luckily enough, word was received by our political leaders in Kinshasa. Mr. Willim Deng, who was the leader of the struggle, had opened some political offices of Sudan African National Union (SANU) in the DRC and some East African countries while South Sudan Liberation Army(SSLA), nicknamed the Nya-nya, or snake poison, was led by General Joseph Lagu who was active in the bush. The Kinshasa office sent one of the politicians to Isiro to intercede on our behalf. Reaching an understanding with the local authorities, our visiting politician asked for clemency from the local authorities. The local authorities were sympathetic and agreed to release us. Having finished our morning duties that day, a meeting was called in which the local dignitaries, our politician, the lawyers, ourselves and the man we attacked were all present. The governor got up to give the speech. He thanked our politician for his visit, the local government employees etc. Admitting that the Congolese government was helping the South Sudanese people in their struggle, he went ahead to announce that we were released, but warned us that we should not take the law into our own hands to harm innocent people. He reported that the man we had beaten was our brother who was very innocent as he was not a Sudan government agent, but somebody who came to visit his sister. Ensuring that our safety was in the hands of the Congolese authorities, he admonished us to desist from doing anything like that again. Our hearts went out to the man we had beaten, as we rushed to him after the meeting and told him how sorry we were. He was very understanding and he told us that he had forgiven us for the wrong we had done to him. We also went to his sister and husband to express our sadness for our wrong deed and they also showed some understanding to our relief.

Soon after our release from prison, the authorities opened big refugee camps in two of the provinces bordering Sudan, including Uele. Our camp was about 15 km. from town in a big thick forest. We were given hoes, machetes, inter alia to clean up our place and build our huts with grass. We also planted a lot of maize, peanuts, yams, cassava and lots of vegetables and some grain and millets. With our UN food, we had more than enough to eat. We took some of our produce to Saturday markets to sell for money to buy other things like meat, soap, salt etc. We were told that guns will be brought to us soon, and so every morning we had strenuous physical exercises to prepare us for any military training that we would undergo to be soldiers. Our hopes were very high and we thought that one day we shall be turned into strong soldiers to fight for our freedom. The same thing was happening in the refugee camps in the other provinces.

One day we had a visit from the leader of our struggle, Mr. William Deng Nhial. He came with a big van all covered up and we thought our guns had arrived. It was about 10:00am. He made us stand in a long line, from the youngest to the oldest. Then he made the 18/19- year olds stand on their own and those of years 20 and above were separated in their row line. Distributing the machetes and other sharp knives for cutting things to those who were 20 years and above, he said to all of us that our problem is not understood in the world, so nobody gave me any guns. With these machetes we shall begin our war of liberation and with other sharp knives was for cutting any wild meat you might find in the way to eat. They were to start immediately to attack the isolated police posts at the border. Any guns got would be availed to the trained soldiers. He ordered that any moving military convoy between towns or provinces must be attacked. Those with the machetes would hide themselves near the road while those soldiers with guns would climb the trees not far from the road and the job of those with the guns was to kill one or two drivers in the middle of the convoy and stop shooting and leave the area. When this happened there would be confusion and those with the machetes who were so many would just rush unexpectedly to attack the army with machetes while others would snatch anything of value they put their hands on such as guns, boxes of bullets and any food item inter alia and run to different directions. Then he turned to us the 18/19-year olds. Saying that he had no money and scholarships to educate us, he told us to go and look for our educational possibilities wherever we found them and that by the time you had finished you would return with the trained mines to help us achieve our liberation struggle. This was the end of our camp. The following morning those with the machetes left to begin the war and those of us also left to look for education while William Deng left for the other refugee camps to do the same as he did to us. The camp was left as a ghost place. We had informed earlier some local Congolese friends whose villages were nearer to us that a day would come when we have to vacate the camp and that when that day came, they should take over the ownership of the place with everything in it. We hoped that after our departure, some of them must have just done that because we left a lot of farm crops unharvested.

CHAPTER THREE

The Search for Education

LEAVING THE CAMP, I went to Isiro and stayed with an American missionary I had met earlier when we were in town. I cut grass and attended flowers in his garden and in return, he provided feeding and accommodation for me, at least for sometimes. I was thinking of what to do: Start learning French language and join school later in DRC or go to East Africa, especially Uganda, where I could continue with my education if I could get admitted into any school. Weighing the pros and cons, between the two choices, I took the latter because learning a new language would have delayed me in advancing my education. While in Isiro, I met a Shilluk boy called Odhok who had the same dilemma like me and had also decided to go to Uganda to look for school.

Having less money for a bus journey, we decided to walk the almost 400km distance between Isiro and Aru, a Congolese town, the HQs of Aru District, at the border with Uganda. The journey was really very exciting as we walked all day just talking about the politics of Sudan and how we day-dreamed that our gallant Anya-nya soldiers would fight with government forces which they would defeat and get our

ESCAPE FROM THE SECURITY FORCES OF THE SUDANESE GOVERNMENT

freedom. Feeling hunger pangs from time to time, we would buy some fresh peanuts and some bananas to eat on the way. To our surprise, most farmers never accepted our money and instead wanted to give us these food items free, saying that we were young students from another country without enough money to feed ourselves. In the evening, we would just enter any house by the roadside and asked for a place to sleep. Not only would they provide us with the accommodation, but they would also give us some food and treated us as members of their family as we would eat with them. This was the same scenario throughout our journey. We had never witnessed anywhere this kind of generosity and pure kindness which touched us greatly. Sometimes, we would spend two or three days in a home where we were excessively well received to help them in their farm work. When time came to leave, the lady of the house with her husband would provide us with a lot of food items: Cooked cassava filled with peanut/sesame butter, bananas, roasted g/nuts, sesame/peanut butter put in a big container for our use on the way inter alia. The man of the house would accompany us for two to three kilometres before bidding us farewell.

It took us three and half weeks (3½) to reach Aru town near the Uganda border. There were some south Sudanese refugees housed by one of the churches in town. We put up with them for some time. After two weeks, my comrade Odhok left for Kampala to look for school while I had decided to look for school in Arua, the HQs of West Nile District of Uganda just 14 miles or 22.4km. from Aru. I heard later that Odhok found school in Kampala. One day he went for holiday to his home village, near Malakal town, South Sudan when things had improved a little and he thought that it was safe for him to go home. Unfortunately, things got hot again while he was in Sudan and one day he was gunned down by security forces in his own village. One day I thought of going

THE SEARCH FOR EDUCATION

to visit Arua town of Uganda. My clothes were torn: my trousers and shirt were torn and was going barefoot. While in Aru, I heard the information that there was one Anglican Mission Secondary School called Mvara Senior Secondary School in Arua. I had decided to go to that school to apply. One night I washed my torn clothes very clean and in the following morning, at around 6:00am, I left for Arua town. Reaching the town at around 10:00am, I went to the school compound. First I went to the well, where I drank water as I was very thirsty, washed my feet that were full of dust and found the office of the Head Master. It happened that an English lady was the Head Mistress, called Miss Loyd. She asked me what I wanted. I told her I was a refugee from Sudan and that I had finished first year in Rumbek secondary school and I showed her my student Identity card. She was a compassionate woman. Telling me to sit under the mango tree outside, she had a meeting with her colleagues and decided to give me tests in English language and Mathematics. Having set these tests, they invited me to the office and told me to sit these tests. Surprisingly, I had no choice, but to sit the tests. I scored these tests in the 90's out of 100 marks).

The teachers were surprised with my high scores and recommended that I be accepted in 3rd year because the second year was full. That was January 1964. Seeing this as a big challenge, I had to work very hard and to my surprise, I found myself heading the class for the rest of academic year. In 1965, I sat for "O level" Cambridge Examinations which I passed with distinctions. The following year, 1966, I joined "A Level" or Advanced Level in Ntare School in Mbarara, Western Uganda. There I met the future leaders of Uganda and Rwanda (of course, we didn't know at the time that they would be leaders of their respective countries): Mr. Yoweri Museveni of Uganda was in the sixth form and Mr. Paul Kigame of Rwanda was in 4th Form and I was in the 5th. Form. I sat my

ESCAPE FROM THE SECURITY FORCES OF THE SUDANESE GOVERNMENT

"Advanced Level" Cambridge Examinations in December 1967 which I passed well and was admitted to the Faculty of Economics, Makerere University in Uganda. Being a refugee, I couldn't enter as I didn't have any scholarship. While we were students, we were hearing about the successes of our brothers in arms. They were doing very well, although no country was helping us. While I was doing my secondary education in Uganda, I was in contact with my friend, colleague and classmate in Rumbek secondary, Mr.John Garang de Mabior, the future leader of South Sudan, was in Grinnell College, Iowa, USA at the time. He had arranged a scholarship for me.

On January 23rd. 1968, I was on a Lufthansa plane on my way to the U.S to start my college education in Grinnell college. Reaching New York City, I was stunned on what I saw: Huge skyscrapers, planes standing in lines like taxis and once filled with the passengers they would take-off inter alia. Somebody from the University of Chicago was to pick me up from the airport. He came and took me to his apartment. In the following morning, he took me to the railway station to finish the rest of my journey by train to Grinnell town. Travelling by train across America was a telling story. I saw beautiful farms, big towns and small towns and I had a feeling that I was in another Planet because where I came from was really very, very different from what I was seeing. Arriving Grinnell in the afternoon, I saw my friend and colleague, Mr. John Garang de Mabior waiting to pick me up from the station. I got down from the train, we embraced each other, a Sudanese form of greeting, took my luggage and we headed for the dormitories where he took me to my room that he booked for me for the second semester. When the college closed for summer holidays in June 1968, we went to the State of Minnesota where we were employed by the State Ministry of Agriculture as weed killers. Armed with big containers full of toxin liquid tied to our backs

THE SEARCH FOR EDUCATION

and equipped with spraying gear, we would walk between the farms and sprayed on these dangerous weeds like thistles inter alia that are inimical to crops. Equipped with a car, we were moving across the state and worked on the farms from Mondays—Fridays. According to employment agreement with the State and us (we were many college students), we had paid accommodation in the field. After work, we just went to any nearby town, found rooms, Monday—Thursdays, spent our nights there paid by the state and then went to our apartments over the weekends to re-start every Monday. We had put up with a very Good Samaritan American family called the Castles that was a strong supporter of South Sudanese people. Returning to College at the beginning of the fall in September 1968 with a saved sum of $1500, we felt we would be financially well-off during the academic year when going out on weekends for the movies and the payment for other miscellaneous items not covered by the scholarship. I had a wonderful academic year doing well in my classes.

In June 1969, John graduated at the top of his class in Grinnell College and was awarded $10,000 for his Ph.D research. He decided to go to university of Dar-e-Salam to study Ujamaa system that the then President Malimu Nyerere had just introduced as an African form of socialism to solve the problem of food insecurity. After graduation, John left for Africa and joined university of Dar-as-salam for his research. Having finished his research in Tanzania, he decided to go to the bush to see how Any-nya forces were doing before returning to the US for his doctoral studies. He found that things were not really good. He decided to join. His performance was so good that some of the senior officers were rumoured to be jealous of him and wanted to do him some harm, but he survived the ordeal. When the Addis-Ababa peace accord was signed in March 1972, he was absorbed into the Sudanese Army as a captain. After sometimes, he was sent to more military training in Georgia, U.S.A. There were 8,000 military officers from many countries in the world, including some officers from the U.S.A, being trained high military tactics and many other military tactics. At the end of the training, comprehensive examinations were given and John Garang became number 2(two) out of 8,000 military officers, a man from Latin America was number one (1). Many Sudanese officers who went with him were at the bottom.

As far as I was concerned, I was invited by an American student friend to go with him to his home town of Portland in Oregon State for my summer vacation with him. While there with him, he found me a job with Georgia Pacific Lumber Company where I worked for the whole summer. It was a very satisfying summer experience and I also came to like the State with a pleasant climate compared to very cold winters in Iowa State where Grinnell is situated. I made a decision to transfer to Oregon State University in the fall of 1969, so I applied and was admitted to study Agricultural Economics under Emery Castle, a well-known Agricultural economist in the U.S. In June, 1971, I graduated with a B.Sc. (Agricultural Economics degree. While Applying for graduate school in Oregon State University, I continued to work with Georgia Pacific Lumber Co. during the 1971 summer holiday since I had become known there and got myself some good friends. In the fall of 1971, I started my graduate studies in the university and in June In1972, I graduated with a M.Sc. (Agriculture Economics, non-Thesis option).

In the summer of 1972, I continued to work with Georgia Pacific Lumber Company in Eugene, Oregon, where I had relocated from Corvallis, the seat of Oregon State university. I worked there for two years on an assembly line. In March 1975, I finally returned to my country, where I worked for some time with an NGO called Sudan

THE SEARCH FOR EDUCATION

Council of Churches (SCC) as Projects officer for this organisation. My job was to write some projects for funding for the churches in Sudan. By September, 1977, I became Teaching Assistant (T.A) in the College of Social and Economic Studies (CSES) of the University of Juba, Sudan. Being sent to France as a government scholar for doctoral studies, I obtained my doctorate (which they call in French doctorat d'universite) in March 1985. Returning to my mother University, I was appointed Lecturer in CSES, Juba University. Over the years I progressed to become Ass. Professor.

While I was still in the States, John Garang had come to the U.S. for military training, as mentioned above. He was anxious to know how I was faring. I went to visit him in Georgia. Meeting again, we exchanged very important views, as he said that there was a good possibly of another war in Sudan as the Numeiri's government was behaving strangely in regard to the Addis-Ababa Accord. He was happy that I had progressed much in my education and that I was heading home. After my visit had ended, we parted promising to meet again in Sudan. Soon after, I left for the Sudan. On coming back from his military training, he returned to the Army. Having done well the assignments that were given to him, he received promotions until he reached the rank of Colonel. After this brilliant military service, he was released for his doctoral studies. He was admitted to do his doctorate in Iowa State University at Ames Iowa. At the end of his doctoral studies, he wrote an excellent thesis on development, based on his research on Ujamaa. Having finished his doctoral studies successfully he returned to the Sudan where he escaped again to the bush on 16th. May1983 to start another liberation war, SPLA/SPLM. This war eventually brought the liberation of South Sudan. This has made Deng Nhial's words to be apocalyptic when he told us in the camp that those going for education would come back with big brains to help us get liberation from our oppressors. It had exactly happened as Deng Nhial said it.

In the early 1990's Sudan was going through a lot of political turbulence and the country was very unstable as Sudan People's Liberation Army & Sudan People's Liberation Movement(SPLA/SPLM) was fighting for the New Sudan. Invited to present a paper in the Arab Economic Conference in Baghdad, Iraq in1994, I went to attend this Conference, but never returned to Sudan and after the conference, I proceeded to Eritrea where SPLA/M had offices. I joined the movement immediately and instead of going for military training, my colleague, Dr.John Garang deMabior, now the leader of SPLA/M, advised me that I was already advanced in age for military service, that I should look for a job, bring my family from Sudan and from time to time I should engage in SPLM conferences to help in mental work, instead of being a soldier. Luckily enough, I got a job with the Ministry of Agriculture of the State of Eritrea in the section of Irrigation. It was a very challenging work and I really liked it. We made important milestones in planning a comprehensive irrigation system for the country. While working in Asmara, Eritrea, I planned to bring my family from Sudan and I succeeded in having my family joined me in Eritrea in 1996. By 1997, I joined World Vision International Sudan Programme stationed in Nairobi (WVI—SP). My job was to write projects to finance our various operations in the liberated areas of South Sudan. We were providing food for the hunger-stricken population in the former Bahr-el-ghazal Province, especially in Tonj and Gogrial areas which were really hard hit by the 1998 hunger/famine. The food airlifts made by WVI-SP from lokochokio to certain locations in Gogrial and Tonj States would be likened to the US food airlifts to West Berlin after the 2nd. World War. Huge cargo planes (6 to 8 of them or even more) full of food items would start their journey at

THE SEARCH FOR EDUCATION

around 6:00am from Lochochokio to go and drop food in those areas and return for another trip. This would continue the whole day until 6:00pm in the evening. The food drops were sometimes dangerous. I remember, I was staying in one of our camps in Apuk Giir Thik area where a lot of food drops were taking place. One day the planes came and made a lot of food drops. People were told to allow the planes to finish dropping food first before they would rush to the fields. Some of them never heeded the advice. One afternoon about four cargos came and began dropping food items, some people rushed to get for themselves some bags and when they rushed to the field, there were so many bags in the air falling, and some of them fell on two people who were crushed to death. While food was being dropped to be distributed to the hungry people, WVI-S? was slaughtering about 12 bulls daily to help those who were dying. We employed ladies to cut the meat of 12 bulls into big lumps, boil it with a lot of onions in around 9 big barrels to make thick soup. When it was ready, we employed another group of women to scoop this soup with a big cup and one piece of meat. Each of them would rush to one person lying down and would make the person drink the soup and eat the piece of meat. In that way we were saving around 100 people a day from starving to death. There was also a lot of porridge being made to be given to those on the point of death.

In the year 2000, SPLM had problems with some NGOs, such as WVI which were expelled from the area. They were to return to the area much later on. While I was working as a consultant with other NGOs, I had applied for resettlement in Australia being helped by Sanctuary, an Organisation that helps refugees, based in Armidale, NSW. By 2004 I was accepted to come to Australia with my family, my wife and five kids. We are now naturalised citizens of Australia. I am now professor emeritus staying in Australia as my home. Sometimes I go alone to my original country, stay for sometimes and come back to Australia. I feel very lucky to have two beautiful countries where I can stay.

CHAPTER FOUR

Conclusion

This is a concluding chapter where we summarise the suffering of the people of South Sudan. From time Immemorial, the people of the South have had a lot of rough time. The Turks tried to take our country and our people defended their territory to the point that the Turks really never had a foothold in the South, as the Turks colonisation only concentrated in the North. On killing General Gordon who was in the service of the Khedive of Egypt, the Mahdi had liberated North Sudan from the Egyptian rule. The next 13 years (1885—1898) saw the emergence of the El Mahdi State, the firs strong Islamic government in the country. During his period, this government tried to conquer the South and Islamize it, but the people of the South resisted successfully. This Mahdi State did not last long enough, because in 1898, Britain launched an invasion to conquer the Sudan as a revenge for killing General Gordon. With this invasion, Sudan came under the British rule for 58 years, after which, the people of the South were simply left to the mercy of Muslims in the North of the country.

The suffering that the people of the South underwent at the hands of Muslims is the basis of this story recounted above. The ordeal cost the people of the South between 3 to 4 million people who died during half a century of struggle from 1955 to 2005. These are just rough estimates because nobody really knows how many southerners died during this period. Because those people who died during escaping forms a good percentage of the total deaths mentioned above, survivors must tell the story. This form of suffering was particularly acute as you may sense it from the story retold above. Our story was good as nobody died. But those who died due to: drowning; eaten by lions, snakes, leopards, all forms of diseases, or by the pangs of hunger inter alia; If those who died were to tell their story you would be weeping.

NB: I do not need to make any references because this is a story telling. The factual material that is found in the introduction, the concluding chapter, and in other parts of the story is, either what I lived/experienced myself e.g. the Torit Mutiny when it happened in 1955, I was in Primary 3 at Akot Elementary school or found in the internet such as the material about the history of Sudan

Printed by Libri Plureos GmbH in Hamburg, Germany